P9-DVY-282

THE ILIAD

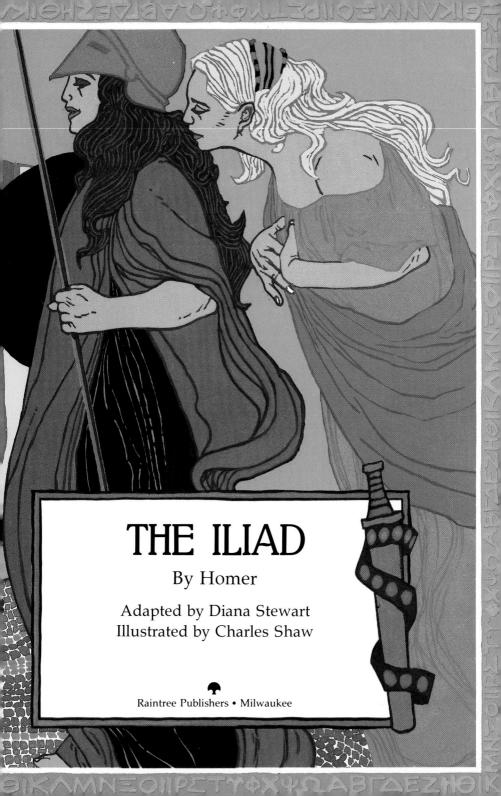

THE ILIAD

By Homer

Adapted by Diana Stewart
Illustrated by Charles Shaw

Raintree Publishers • Milwaukee

Copyright © 1981, Raintree Publishers Inc.

All rights reserved. No part of this book may be
reproduced or utilized in any form or by any means,
electronic or mechanical, including photocopying,
recording, or by any information storage and retrieval
system, without permission in writing from the Publisher.
Inquiries should be addressed to Raintree Publishers Inc.,
310 West Wisconsin Avenue, Milwaukee, Wisconsin 53203.

Library of Congress Number: 80-15669

8 9 10 11 12 13 14 15 16   90 89 88

Printed and bound in the United States of America

Library of Congress Cataloging in Publication Data

Stewart, Diana.
   The Iliad.

   (Raintree short classics)
   SUMMARY: Retells in simple language the events of
the war between Greece and the city of Troy,
focusing on Achilles' quarrel with Agamemnon.
   [1. Mythology, Greek. 2. Troy — Fiction]
I. Homerus. Ilias. II. Shaw, Charles, 1941-
III. Title. IV. Series.
PZ8.1.S8573Il   883'.01   82-15669
ISBN 0-8172-1663-4 (lib. bdg.)
ISBN 0-8172-2011-9 softcover

CONTENTS

PROLOGUE

No city was greater or more powerful than the city of Troy. The king of Troy — King Priam — ruled wisely and well. The people of Troy, the Trojans, were happy, and the king was happy too because he had many fine sons. One son was Hector, a great man and a mighty warrior. Another was Paris, young and handsome.

One day three goddesses came to Paris. First was Hera, wife of Zeus, the chief of all the gods. Second was Athena, a fierce goddess who loved the excitement of war. And third was Aphrodite, the goddess of love and beauty. Paris, of course, was amazed to see them. He was even more amazed when each of the goddesses offered him a prize. He had only to choose which gift he thought was the best.

Hera offered to make him the ruler over all Europe and Asia. Athena promised to make him a great warrior who would defeat the Greeks. Aphrodite offered to give him the most beautiful woman in the world for his own.

Now Paris did not want to be a great ruler, nor did he want to be a great warrior. But he loved beauty, and he chose Aphrodite's gift. This offended Hera and Athena, and they left in anger.

Everyone knew that the most beautiful woman in all the world was Helen, the wife of Menelaus, the king of the city of Sparta. And Aphrodite took Paris to Greece to claim his prize. When Paris arrived in Sparta, Menelaus welcomed him as a guest. The Spartan king, of course, did not know that Paris planned to rob him of his wife.

After several days, Menelaus had to leave Sparta on a journey, but he left his guest in his wife's care. In those few days, Helen fell in love with Paris. When Menelaus returned, Paris had gone — taking Helen and many great riches with him back to Troy.

King Menelaus was enraged! He called all the chief

princes of Greece to him and asked for their help. Together, he said, they would destroy Troy and bring Helen back.

Among the great warriors who went with Menelaus were his brother Agamemnon; Achilles, the greatest and bravest of all warriors; and the wise Odysseus, King of Ithaca. The Greeks gathered an army of thousands of men and ships and set sail for Troy.

From Mount Olympus — home of the gods — the gods and goddesses saw all that had happened, and they took sides. Hera and Athena, who were still angry with Paris, vowed to help the Greeks. Aphrodite and Apollo, who loved beauty, vowed to help the Trojans.

And so the Trojan War began.

THE QUARREL

1

For nine years the Greeks and the Trojans fought. The battle favored first one side and then the other. But at the beginning of the tenth year, the Greeks began to fight among themselves. This is the way the trouble began.

An army of Greeks led by the great king Agamemnon left the shores of Troy to capture another city, Thebes. They sacked the city, taking with them the treasures to be divided among the warriors. They also took with them two women. Chryseis — the daughter of the priest of Thebes — was given to Agamemnon as his prize. Briseis — a girl of great beauty and charm — was given to Achilles.

Chryseis's father came to Agamemnon to pay a ransom and take his daughter back, but Agamemnon refused to let her go.

"She is mine," he said. "And I will keep her. I will take her home with me. Now, say no more! Leave me before I become angry. Let me never see your face again!"

The priest was frightened and left, but he walked to the shores of the sea and prayed to the god Apollo.

"Oh, Apollo! Hear me! I have always shown you honor and respect. I have prayed to you and sent burnt offerings to you. Help me now! Help me get Chryseis back. And make the Greeks pay for the pain and sorrow they have caused me!"

Apollo heard his priest, and he was angry. He took his silver bow and a quiver of arrows and sat down on a hill above the Greeks' camp. One by one he shot his arrows.

He shot at the men and the animals. All around they dropped to the ground dead. For nine days he shot his deadly arrows.

On the tenth day, Hera — who had been watching Apollo — called Achilles to her. "Achilles, you must do something, or your army will surely die. Call in a prophet and find out why this plague has come upon you."

And Achilles did as Hera told him. He gathered what was left of the army and asked the prophet to explain what they had done to anger Apollo.

"Apollo is angry," spoke the prophet, "because the Greeks have insulted his priest. Agamemnon would not accept the ransom he offered for his daughter. Apollo will not stop the plague until Chryseis is returned to her father without ransom."

Agamemnon was enraged when he heard these words. "What?" he said. "I am to give back my prize and have nothing? I do not want my men to suffer, however. I will give the girl back, but the Greeks must give me something in return. It is not right that I should be the only one without a prize."

"Agamemnon," Achilles pleaded, "how can the Greeks give you a prize? We have little. The treasure has already been divided. But if you give up the girl Chryseis, surely the gods will bless you. And we will repay you four times over when the city of Troy falls."

"Achilles," replied Agamemnon angrily, "do not try to make a fool of me! You expect me to give back the girl and have nothing? I will give the girl back, but I will take your prize instead — the lovely Briseis!"

"I have heard enough!" raged Achilles. "You are selfish and greedy. Why should my men and I follow you as a leader? We came with you to Troy as a favor. We have nothing against the Trojans. No! When Paris stole your sister-in-law Helen, I came with you to avenge the wrong done to Menelaus. I did not come to be insulted by you! Now I will no longer stay. I would rather take my men

and ships and return home than fight to gain more wealth for you!"

"Then leave, Achilles!" Agamemnon replied. "I do not beg you to stay. I have others just as brave and strong to fight! I will take Briseis from you. Then all men will see that I am not afraid of your threats!"

Achilles could not bear this insult. He had his sword half-drawn when Athena came to his side and stopped his hand. Achilles alone could see her — for she made herself invisible to all others.

"Oh, Athena," cried Achilles, "why do you stop me? You have heard Agamemnon insult me!"

"Achilles," the goddess replied, "Hera sent me. Do not fight with Agamemnon. If you control your temper now, you will later have gifts heaped upon you. Wound him with your words but not with your sword."

And Achilles obeyed the goddess. He turned on Agamemnon with his eyes blazing. "Agamemnon, you sit in your tent drinking your wine, lusting after wealth, but you do not have the courage of a dog. Go back to your battles, and when the mighty Hector slays the army of Greece and desperately you need me — I will not be there. Then you will see the result of your greed!"

After Achilles had gone, Agamemnon fulfilled his promise to return the woman Chryseis to her father and put an end to Apollo's anger. He then fulfilled his second promise and sent two servants to Achilles's ship to take Briseis away from the mighty warrior. The men stood before Achilles, embarrassed and afraid, but he called to them:

"Come in, my friends. You have nothing to fear from me. I know that you only obey Agamemnon's orders. But watch and see! The king shall be punished for his greed and the wrong he has done me!"

After the servants left with the lovely Briseis, Achilles wept bitter tears. He had loved the girl and wanted her for his wife. He prayed to his mother Thetis. She was a sea-spirit and a favorite of Zeus. Thetis heard her son and left the gray mist of the sea to come to him. Gently she held him in her arms and said, "Why are you weeping, Achilles? Speak and share your sorrow with me."

"Mother," answered Achilles, "you are wise and know the insult Agamemnon has paid me. He has taken away my prize. Now I ask your help. Go to Zeus. Beg him to aid the Trojans in battle. When our Greek soldiers lie dead on the battlefield, Agamemnon will know the price he has paid for the wrong he did me. He will know that I am a warrior to be honored and respected."

"My child," his mother replied, "my heart weeps for you. I will go to Zeus and plead for his help."

And Zeus listened to Thetis and promised his support. That night he went to Agamemnon in a dream and lied to the king. He told him that the time had come for the Greeks to have their victory over the Trojans. He told Agamemnon to gather all his armies together and attack Troy.

The next morning, Agamemnon rallied his soldiers together to attack the Trojan army. And as the morning mist cleared, the two armies faced each other. But before the hard fighting began, Paris stepped out from the ranks. He challenged the Greeks to send out their best warrior to fight him alone. This duel would put an end to the war without killing more of their men. Whoever was the winner could claim the victory for his own side. If Paris won, Helen would stay in Troy and the Greeks would return home. If the Greek warrior won, Helen would be returned along with prizes of great wealth.

The Greeks listened to Paris and agreed to his terms. No sooner did Menelaus hear the challenge than he leaped from his chariot in full armor ready to do battle with Paris. But when Paris saw him, his courage failed him. He would have fled, but his brother Hector stopped him.

"Paris!" roared Hector. "You are the cause of all this trouble. For your sake have our soldiers fought and died. Now you have made the challenge, and you cannot turn back! Your own people would despise you. The Greeks

would laugh at this prince of Troy who runs from Menelaus."

Paris was ashamed of his own cowardice and said to Hector: "You are right, brother. I will fight. But let each side swear a solemn oath that whichever side wins, it will be an end to the fighting. From then on the Trojans and the Greeks will live in faith and friendship."

Both sides agreed to the terms of the battle, and the armies put down their swords and spears. Paris and Menelaus stood alone in the middle of the battlefield. They would fight until one or the other was dead.

THE DUEL BETWEEN PARIS AND MENELAUS

2

From high above the battlefield on the wall of Troy, the beautiful Helen looked down on Paris and Menelaus. She loved the handsome Paris, but her heart ached also for Menelaus and for her city of Sparta and her parents there. King Priam called to her.

"Come, Helen. Sit here by me. You know that I do not blame you for the suffering that has befallen Troy. No one is to blame but the gods."

"King Priam," Helen replied, "I wish I had died before this trouble came upon me. Now I cry my life away."

Meanwhile, the Trojan Hector and the Greek Odysseus marked off the spot for the duel. Into a helmet they put two stones — one for Paris and one for Menelaus. They would shake the helmet until a stone jumped out. That warrior would have the right to throw his spear first.

When all was ready, they shook the helmet. Out leaped Paris's stone.

The armies of both sides grew silent. Taking careful aim, Paris hurled his long spear straight at Menelaus. But his spear struck the king's shield and did not pierce it. Now it was Menelaus's turn to throw.

"Great Zeus," he prayed, "help me to punish Paris for his crimes!" And he threw his spear with such mighty force that it pierced the shield of Paris and tore through the armor breastplate. Paris, however, turned with a sudden movement. And the spear went to one side of his body.

When Menelaus saw that he had missed, he threw him-

16

self upon Paris and grabbed him by the strap of his helmet. Twisting it tightly, he began to drag the choking Paris toward the line of Greek soldiers.

Now Paris would have surely died, but Aphrodite was watching over him. She made the strap break in Menelaus's hands. And before he could recover and grab Paris again, she whisked the prince away in a cloud and delivered him back behind the walls of Troy — to the rooms he shared with Helen.

There Helen found him. She knew that Aphrodite had saved his life, and she was jealous of the beautiful goddess. In a rage she turned on Paris. "Paris," she said, "I wish you were dead! You have bragged for so long that you were a better man than my husband. But if it hadn't been for Aphrodite, Menelaus would have killed you!"

Paris did not get angry with Helen, for he loved her. Instead he calmed her and wooed her until she held him again with loving arms. "Do not worry, my love," he said gently. "You are still mine. The war is not yet over. We still have gods on our side."

And, indeed, the gods and goddesses on Mount Olympus had watched the duel with great interest. Menelaus had clearly won the fight, and the Greeks should have been given the victory. But Athena and Hera were not satisfied to see the war end so easily. They wanted to see Troy destroyed, and they made a plan.

Down Athena went from Olympus to Troy. There she found a warrior with his bow and arrow. "Soldier," she said, "you are a great archer. I dare you now to shoot Menelaus down — there where he stands. Think of the glory that will be yours. Prince Paris will be so grateful that he will shower you with rich gifts."

The poor fool of an archer listened to Athena's words. He drew back his bow and let his arrow fly straight toward Menelaus. But it was not part of Athena's plan to have the arrow kill the king. She flew to Menelaus's side before the deadly arrow arrived and brushed it aside so that it hit his belt buckle first and wounded him only a little. But from the small wound, blood gushed forth.

Agamemnon was enraged by what the Trojans had done to his brother. He vowed that he would not stop the fighting now until the entire city of Troy lay in ruins.

The Greeks now fought with a new strength. They were led by the mighty warrior Diomedes. King Diomedes was second only to Achilles in bravery and daring. He raged through the Trojan lines, killing all before him.

Now next to Hector, the mightiest Trojan was Prince Aeneas. He was the mortal son of Aphrodite herself. He and his friend Pandarus fought side by side. Together they attacked Diomedes. Pandarus took his spear and threw it. The spear passed through Diomedes's shield and into the armor, but the point did not pierce his body. Pandarus, however, cried: "You are a dead man, Diomedes! And the glory for killing you will be mine!"

"You missed, Pandarus!" Diomedes answered, and he let fly his spear with such force that it tore through the man's face. Pandarus fell from his chariot — dead.

Aeneas leaped down to rescue his friend's body. He yelled like a lion, ready to kill anyone who came near him. Diomedes had no spear now, but he picked up a giant rock and threw it at Aeneas, crushing his hip and leg. The prince dropped to the ground, and he surely would have been killed if Aphrodite had not arrived. She gathered her son up in her arms and would have taken him away, but Diomedes saw her. Picking up a spear, he aimed well and struck the goddess in the hand. Her immortal blood ran from the cut, and she cried in pain and fear, dropping her son to the ground.

"Stay away from the battle, Aphrodite," Diomedes called. "You are a feeble woman. Stick to your loving and leave the fighting to your stronger sisters!" And Aphrodite fled back to Olympus, whimpering in pain.

With a cry, Diomedes charged down on the fallen Aeneas and would have finished the work he had begun

with the rock, but Apollo was watching. He took the prince away from Diomedes and back within the walls of Troy.

And the battles raged on. First one side would win and then the other. Many great warriors on both sides were killed.

No one fought more bravely than Hector. He raged through the battlefield, leaving death and destruction behind him. With Achilles gone, there was no one to equal him.

One night he returned home to his wife Andromache. He found her holding their son and weeping. "Oh, Hector," she cried. "Can you not stop this fighting? How long can you live through these bloody battles? Do you want to see me a widow and your son an orphan? Stay! Stay with me!"

"Andromache," Hector said gently, "how could I face my men if I sent them into battle and stayed here safe with you? And how long would we be safe? I know that Troy is doomed. As surely as I live, I must fight and die. Nothing can stop my fate."

Tenderly he held his child in his arms. "I pray to Zeus," he said, "that when my son grows to be a man and goes into battle, men will say: 'Hector's son is even mightier than his father!' "

Gently he drew Andromache to him and held her close. "My poor love," he said, "men were made to fight and die. I must be first in danger just as I am first in glory."

And Hector left her weeping. She mourned him while he was still alive, because she feared she would never see him again.

GIFTS FOR ACHILLES

3

As the war continued its bloody path, Zeus remembered his promise to Thetis. He would aid the Trojans. And when Hector returned to battle, he was braver and fiercer than ever.

All this time, Achilles sat in his camp. He would not listen to the cries of the Greeks as they fell to their deaths.

With greater and greater strength the Trojan armies fought. Led by the mighty Hector, they drove the Greek forces back away from the walls of Troy. Before long, they had driven them nearly to the edge of the sea where their ships were anchored. Victory after victory the Trojans won — and the dead Greek warriors covered the battlefield.

At last one night, Agamemnon called his men around him. "We are beaten," he said. "Let us leave now before we are all killed."

But Diomedes refused to listen to these cowardly words. "Agamemnon!" he cried. "Go if you want to. Take your men and ships with you if you are afraid. But for myself, I will stay here and fight until the city of Troy lies in ruins! Justice is on our side. We fight to avenge the wrong done to your brother. And the gods will surely come to help us. Let us ask the prophet Nestor what we must do to turn our defeat into victory."

When he finished speaking, all the men of Greece cheered him. And the great prophet Nestor rose from his place and spoke.

"Diomedes, you are very wise for your young years. Now listen to me, Agamemnon! Listen to what I have to say! The great god Zeus himself gave you the right to rule the Greeks. He gave you his laws that you might rule with wisdom. But you have not been wise. You offended Achilles. You took Briseis, his prize, from him and insulted his honor. You gave in to your own greed and pride."

"Nestor," Agamemnon replied, "what you say is true. What I did was wrong. But now, what can we do?"

"Only Achilles can defeat Hector," the prophet answered. "You must go to him. You must offer him great gifts and beg him to return to battle."

"I was a fool!" the king said. "But now I will do as you say. Oh, men of Greece, here is what I will offer Achilles if he will return. Besides the gold and silver, I will give him a dozen of my best horses. And I will return Briseis to him unharmed. And when we destroy Troy, he shall fill his ship with gold. Twenty women he may choose for his slaves. Also, he may choose one of my own daughters for his wife. Seven of my richest cities I will give him to rule. All these things I will give him if he will join with us once more."

"This is good, King Agamemnon," replied Nestor. "Call your men to gather these gifts. We will send them with the wise Odysseus to plead for you."

When the gifts had been gathered, Odysseus and two of his men went to Achilles's camp. They soon found the great warrior in his tent with his dearest friend, Patroclus. Achilles was playing a lyre and singing. He greeted Odysseus warmly.

"Welcome, Odysseus, my dear friend. Come in. Patroclus! Find meat and drink for our friends."

After they had eaten, Odysseus raised his cup of wine to Achilles. "I drink to your health, my friend, and to your mercy. King Agamemnon has sent me to plead in his behalf. Outside I have gifts of great wealth he offers you — and the lovely maiden Briseis. All these and much more are yours if you will forget the insult he paid you and return with your armies." And Odysseus explained all that Agamemnon had promised.

"Achilles," he continued, "the Trojans are destroying

us. Tomorrow could see the end of our armies. Right now Hector and his men are waiting for morning to come. Then they will burn our ships and leave us helpless. Hector fights like a madman, and no one can stop him. No one but you."

"Odysseus," Achilles replied, "it is too late. Agamemnon cannot buy my loyalty now. For nine years I fought for him. A dozen cities I destroyed and robbed of their riches while he sat safe in his tent. All I won I gave to Agamemnon to divide. He gave some to each of the warriors, but most he kept for himself. And then he took from me the woman I loved with all my heart. So now I am to forgive him because he needs me? I say no! I do not trust him! I do not trust his word. He is greedy and a coward. He has sinned against me and thinks that rich treasures can buy me. Well, I tell you that I would not return to fight if he gave me ten times — no, twenty times — the riches he has offered! I would not marry his daughter if she were more beautiful than Aphrodite herself! My honor means more to me than any wealth or glory! Go back to Agamemnon. Tell him this. Tomorrow my men and I will board our ships and take to the sea. My advice to you is to follow my example. Load your ships and sail for home before you are all killed!"

Odysseus listened to Achilles's bitter words and was silent for a moment. Then he spoke once more. "Achilles, even the gods in their wisdom forgive. Can you do less than forgive Agamemnon? I swear that his repentance is sincere."

"No more, Odysseus! Do not turn my love for you into hatred!"

"Have you no pity, Achilles?" he pleaded. "Have you forgotten how the armies of Greece honor and respect you?"

"No, I have not forgotten — any more than I have forgotten how Agamemnon insulted me in front of all these same Greeks. So go back and give him my answer!"

Thus Odysseus returned to Agamemnon.

"Odysseus," Agamemnon cried. "What answer did Achilles send? Has he agreed to accept the gifts and forgive the wrong I did him?"

"No," Odysseus replied. "He will not accept the gifts. He advises us to load our ships and leave in defeat."

"He is proud, Agamemnon," Diomedes said. "He will not fight until his heart tells him to."

The next day Achilles watched from his camp. He saw his brave countrymen go into the battle for their lives. They fought hard and bravely, but the Trojans — led by Hector — were stronger and mightier still. It seemed as if nothing could stop them. Achilles watched his comrades fall on the battlefield. His curiosity grew too strong to be contained. At last he called his beloved friend Patroclus to him.

"Patroclus, I must know who of my friends have fallen in battle today. Go down and find the prophet Nestor. Ask him who has been killed or wounded."

Patroclus obeyed Achilles and soon found Nestor nursing the wounded warriors. He told Nestor that he had been sent by Achilles, and Nestor said: "Why does Achilles want to know of our wounded? He does not care that our brave Greeks die because he has deserted them. If he cared, he would forget his anger and fight with them. Is he waiting until our ships have all been burned, and death is our fate? Tell him that Diomedes was wounded today. Tell him that Odysseus and Agamemnon have been wounded and can no longer fight! Speak to him, Patroclus! See if he will listen to you — for he loves you above all other men."

And Patroclus's heart was touched by Nestor's words. "I will try, Nestor, but I am afraid that his pride will stop him from coming to help you."

"Then," said Nestor, "if he will not come himself, you put on his armor. The Greeks will think you are Achilles, and they will find new courage. The Trojans — seeing you — will be afraid. That is our only hope left now."

PATROCLUS ENTERS THE BATTLE

4

When Patroclus returned to Achilles, tears of sorrow ran down his face. "What are these tears, Patroclus?" asked Achilles. "You cry like a child? What news have you heard?"

"Oh, Achilles, you would not blame me for my tears if you saw what I had seen. Diomedes, Odysseus, and Agamemnon all lie wounded and unable to fight. The Trojans have nearly reached the ships. If help does not come to our armies, the Trojans will surely burn the ships. Then there will be no escape from death. If you will not help your people, let me go in your place! Give me your armor to wear. Let me join the fight and bring new hope to the Greeks. The Trojans are tired, but I am fresh. I can drive them back away from the ships."

Achilles was moved by his friend's words. "All right, Patroclus," he said at last. "I said I would not fight myself unless my own ships were in danger, but you may take my armor and join the battle. But Patroclus, listen to my words! Listen and obey — for your life depends on it."

And these were Achilles's words: "Go, Patroclus, and save the ships from the Trojans. But when you have done this, come back to me. Do not try to fight Hector. Fight for the ships, but do not follow the Trojans back toward the city! The god Apollo protects the walls of Troy."

Even as the two men spoke, Hector led his army closer and closer to the first ship. The Greek warrior Ajax fought bravely for his ship. But blow after blow fell on his shield.

He panted with weariness and sweat poured down his body. Finally Hector himself attacked Ajax and drove the brave Greek away.

At once the Trojans set fire to the ship. The flames leaped over the hull and along the decks. Achilles and Patroclus saw the flames and smoke shooting into the air.

"Come, Patroclus," Achilles cried. "Put on my armor, and I will gather my men together to go with you. The Trojans must not burn any more ships!"

Quickly Patroclus donned the armor of bronze and silver. On his head he put the plumed helmet. While he did this, Achilles rallied his men — over two thousand in all. "Go, my comrades," he said to them. "Follow Patroclus into battle and show the Trojans your bravery and strength!"

When they had gone, Achilles went into his tent and took from his chest a silver cup. This was the cup he used to pray to Zeus alone. In it he poured a clear wine as an offering to the god. Raising his eyes to the heavens, he prayed:

"Oh, Great God Zeus, hear me! Grant me this prayer. Go with Patroclus into battle. Make his heart strong and brave. Help him drive the Trojans away from the ships, and then bring him back to me safe and unharmed."

And Zeus heard his prayer. He granted Patroclus the victory — but he refused to grant him a safe return.

On Patroclus marched with his army until they reached the battlefield. With a cry they threw themselves upon the Trojan army. When the Greeks saw this brave warrior in Achilles's armor, they believed it was Achilles himself, and it gave them new strength and courage.

With roaring cries the Greeks fought the Trojans back away from the ships. Their swords and spears flashed. Blood gushed from the wounded Trojans. Menelaus and Patroclus fought without tiring. Nothing seemed to stop them. The Trojans were pushed back toward the walls of Troy. Death hovered over them all. The Greeks fought until the Trojans could only retreat with terrified screams.

And Patroclus — forgetting Achilles's orders — followed the retreating army. He followed them clear to the walls of the city. For a time it seemed as if he would conquer the very city of Troy. At the gates of the city Hector jumped from his chariot and faced Patroclus. He had to kill this Greek warrior or the Trojans would surely be defeated.

All this Apollo watched from on high. He watched, and he knew that without his help, Hector would die — for Patroclus fought with the strength of a giant. With the speed of lightning Apollo came down from Olympus. He moved to a place behind Patroclus where the warrior could not see him. Then, with a mighty hand, the god struck Patroclus in the back. Achilles's helmet flew from his head. With another blow, Apollo broke Patroclus's spear and stripped the armored breastplate from him.

There Patroclus stood, dazed and weak. He was unable to move to defend himself. And Hector quickly lunged at him, thrusting his spear through his body.

"So, Patroclus," Hector cried, "you thought you could defeat the Trojans! Now may you lie here until the vultures pick your bones clean!"

"Hector," sighed the dying Patroclus, "brag now of your victory if you will. But remember this. You have not long to live. Already your fate is sealed in heaven. You will die at the hands of Achilles, and not even Apollo can save you then!"

As he finished speaking, his soul flew from his body, and he died at the height of his youth and vigor.

King Menelaus saw Patroclus fall, and before the Trojans could take his body, the king flew to his side. "Leave the body!" he cried. "I will kill any man who tries to take it! Patroclus was brave and noble, and he must receive a proper burial!"

Thus Menelaus spoke, and the gods approved. It was the duty of every man to bury his dead. Without burial the soul could never cross into the kingdom of death and find rest. Instead it would wander alone forever. Not even the gods could save it then.

But even as Menelaus spoke, the Trojan army began to close in on him. If he stayed to fight for Patroclus, he was doomed to death. With a cry he fled. Hector came to the body and began to strip off the glorious armor of Achilles. Joyfully he put it on himself.

From on high, Zeus looked down. "Oh, Hector," the great god said, "you do not think of death, but death is near you. For a while I shall give you victory, but for this you give up your life. Your good wife Andromache will never see you alive in Achilles's stolen armor."

While Hector dressed himself, Menelaus rallied the Greek forces. Bravely they fought. Their one thought now was to save the body of their comrade. At last Menelaus and Ajax stood guard over the naked corpse of Patroclus. The king called one of his warriors to him.

"Go," Menelaus said. "Find Achilles. Tell him what has happened here. Warn him that he must hurry to help us if he would save the body of his beloved friend."

So bravely the Greeks fought on, and there was no rest from the terrible battle.

In his camp Achilles waited for news of Patroclus. In the distance he could see the battle raging, and he feared for his friend's life.

"Oh, Patroclus!" he cried. "I ordered you to come back to me! I warned you not to try to fight the mighty Hector!"

Achilles was crying when the messenger from Menelaus found him. "Oh, Achilles," the warrior moaned. "I bring you bad news. Patroclus is dead, and even now they are fighting for his naked corpse. Hector has stripped him of your armor and is wearing it himself!"

Achilles wept in anger and pain. He tore his hair, and poured dust over his hair and face. His cries were so loud that they reached his mother deep in the waters of the sea. Quickly Thetis hurried to him. "My son," she said. "Tell me why you are crying. Zeus granted your wish, and the Trojans are soundly defeating the Greeks. Agamemnon now knows your true worth."

"Oh, Mother! What good is my honor to me when my beloved friend Patroclus lies dead. Hector has killed him and stripped him of my armor. Even now the Trojan prince wears the plumed helmet and silver shield. I will not rest until I have killed that dog Hector! He has robbed me of the best and most loved of men. Oh, Patroclus!"

"If you kill Hector, my son, your own death will soon follow!"

"I no longer care if I die! Oh, I wish an end to war! Let the gods and man live in peace! I wish an end to hatred and anger that brings such pain and suffering! Anger made me fight with Agamemnon, but that anger is at an end. I will fight the Trojans now, and I will kill Hector. I care nothing for my own fate. Let Zeus and the other gods do what they will."

"My heart aches for you, Achilles," Thetis said. "But grant me this one request. Hector struts and parades before the armies wearing your armor. Do not go into battle until I bring you more armor to protect you."

Achilles saw the wisdom of her words and agreed to wait. After Thetis had done, Hera sent a messenger — the goddess Iris — to him. "Achilles," Iris cried. "Quickly, come with me! Even now Hector is trying to steal Patroclus's body. He would cut off the head and put it on a stake outside the gates of Troy. If you would stop him, you must show yourself to the Trojans. They will run in fear of you, and this will give your comrades a chance to save Patroclus's corpse."

Achilles obeyed the goddess with all speed. He stood near the battle trenches, and Athena sent a blaze of fire around him that shot up toward heaven. He was a terrible sight to behold. When the Greeks saw him, they sent up a cry of joy. The Trojans trembled in fear, and while they were too stunned to fight, Menelaus carried his comrade's body to safety — to the waiting arms of Achilles.

THE DEATH OF HECTOR

5

Hector raged and stormed in his camp that night.

"Hector," his friends said, "Achilles is back! Let us retreat behind the walls of the city and fight him from there."

"Hide if you want to," Hector replied angrily. "As for me, I am not afraid to fight Achilles!"

But even as Hector spoke, Thetis returned to Achilles with the armor that she had had specially made by the God of Fire. The shield was wide and strong, and the breastplate was so thick that no spear could pierce it.

The next morning, dressed in his new armor, Achilles led the Greek army into battle. He fought with the strength of a dozen men. Blood flowed under his sword and spear. He showed no mercy to the Trojans. He cut down the enemy in rage and wild fury.

When he saw Prince Polydorus — Hector's young brother — he charged down from his horse and drove his spear into the back of the boy. Polydorus fell to the ground, the blood of life flowing from his body.

Hector watched his beloved brother fall, and tears came to his eyes. But then they filled with rage. With a cry he threw his spear at Achilles — but he missed. Achilles sprang at him and would have killed him, but Apollo wrapped Hector in a mist. Three times Achilles tried to strike, but each time the cloud stopped him. At last he cried: "You escape me this time, Hector, but we will meet again. The gods will not save you from death then!"

Back Achilles went into battle, more fierce than ever. The

ground ran with Trojan blood. Everywhere the Trojans lay dead from Achilles's swift sword. His armor was splattered with enemy blood; and still he did not stop.

Finally, the Trojans could take no more. They poured into the city to find safety behind the high walls. Hector alone stood outside the gates. From inside his father saw him and called, "Hector! My son! Come into the city! You will be killed!"

Hector did not obey, but he was afraid. As he watched Achilles come closer, he trembled, and then he turned and ran. Three times Achilles chased him around the walls of the city before his courage returned.

"Achilles," he said at last, "before we fight to the death, let us take an oath. Let us vow that whichever of us is killed, the other will give his body back to his friends for a proper burial."

"You are mad!" Achilles cried. "I will swear no oath with you! There is no honor between animals. I am the wolf, and I will slaughter you like a lamb! You will suffer for my friends you have killed! There is no escape for you this time." So saying, he threw his spear — but Hector ducked and the spear flew over his head.

"Did you think your words could frighten me again, Achilles? Did you think to strike me in the back as I ran? Take this, you dog!"

And Hector threw his spear strong and straight, but it hit Achilles's shield and bounced harmlessly away. In a rage the Trojan prince drew his sword and charged Achilles. Bravely he fought, but the armor of the Fire-god protected Achilles.

Hector, however, was still wearing Achilles's old armor — and the Greek warrior knew just the spot that was unprotected by the bronze and silver armor. With a cry Achilles drove his sword into Hector's throat. The blade tore through the neck and came out the other side.

"Hector!" Achilles panted. "This armor you took from my friend Patroclus has been your death!"

"Achilles," gasped Hector, "I beg of you! Give my

body to my beloved father so that it may burn on the funeral fire!"

"Never, Hector! I would not give up your body if your father offered me your weight in gold!"

"Think again, Achilles! Or I shall bring the anger of the gods down upon you!" These were the last words he spoke. Swiftly his soul left the body of the bravest and mightiest of the Trojan warriors.

"Hector," Achilles said to the corpse, "my fate is in the hands of Zeus." And quickly he began removing the stolen armor from Hector's body while the Greek army watched in wonder. When he finished, he grabbed Hector by the ankles. With leather strips he bound them to the back of a chariot so the warrior's head hung behind on the ground. Achilles himself whipped up the horses. On he galloped with Hector's body dragging in a cloud of dust.

From high upon the wall of Troy, King Priam cried and tore at his hair in grief. Andromache ran to the wall in time to see the naked corpse of her husband being dragged away.

"Oh, Hector!" she sobbed. "My beloved! Cruel fate has brought us nothing but pain and misery. You alone kept the city from destruction. Nothing can save us now!" And all the women of Troy added their cries to hers.

Once back in the Greek camp, the warriors mourned the death of Patroclus. While Achilles cried and held his head, each man cut off a lock of hair to cover the body. A great funeral fire was then made to burn the body. Last of all Achilles gathered up the white bones of his beloved friend, wrapped them in linen, put them in a golden urn, and buried them.

For twelve days Achilles mourned the death of his friend. During those days Hector's corpse lay unburied, but the gods protected it from harm. The gods were angry with Achilles. Hector had been a brave and honorable man, and the gods themselves knew he deserved an honorable burial.

At last Zeus called Achilles's mother to him. "Thetis,"

said the great god. "Go to your son. Tell Achilles that the gods are not pleased with this madness in his heart. He sits weeping over the grave of his dead friend, but he will not grant the noble Hector the same honor. It is my command that he give up the body. Tell him that if a ransom is offered, he must accept it."

After Thetis had left to do his bidding, Zeus called Iris to his side. "Iris, go down to Troy. Seek out King Priam. Tell him to gather together great riches. Tell him to take these to the Greek camp — to Achilles. Have him offer this wealth as a ransom for the body of his son."

And Iris, too, went on her way.

Meanwhile, Thetis arrived at the side of weeping son. "Achilles," she said. "I have been sent by Zeus. Listen to me and obey Zeus's commands."

"All right, Mother," he said when she had finished. "I will obey the great god Zeus. If it is his wish, I will accept the ransom for Hector's body."

Priam himself drove the chariot filled with gold and rare treasure. And Zeus protected him so that no Greek dared to harm him. Straight to Achilles's camp Priam drove. When he saw the great warrior, he threw himself at Achilles's feet and kissed his hand.

"Pity me, Achilles," he said. "Pity me and return my son to me. For the ransom I have brought you, give me back the body of my beloved Hector!"

Achilles's heart was touched by the sorrow of this noble king. He drew Priam to his feet. "How great has been your grief," he said. "What horrors you must feel to kiss the hand that killed your sons. You have suffered much since the gods brought this terrible war on your land. Here — sit and rest."

"Do not ask me to rest, oh great Achilles, while the body of my son lies unburied. The ransom is yours. Only take me to his corpse."

But Achilles grew stern. "Sit awhile, old man! Do as I bid you!" And Priam grew afraid and obeyed. But while he sat,

Achilles called his servants to him. He told them to wash the torn and bloody body of Hector and wrap it in clean linen before it was given to his father. When this was done, he returned to Priam.

"Hector's body now lies ready for you. Return with him to Troy. For eleven days our armies will be at peace. During that time you may mourn your son and give him the royal burial that is his right."

The next morning at dawn, King Priam returned to Troy with his dead son and all the city mourned his loss. Beautiful Helen — the cause of all the death and destruction — wept bitter tears. "Oh, Hector!" she cried. "If only I had died before I brought all this pain and death to your city!"

And the worst was yet to come. After eleven days of peace, the truce ended. On the twelfth, the fighting began again. Before the tenth year of the Trojan War passed, the great city lay in burned ruins. Troy was no more.

GLOSSARY OF PROPER NAMES

On the Greek side

Achilles (ə kil' ēz)   the greatest Greek warrior

Agamemnon (ag' ə mem' non)   a Greek leader, brother of Menelaus

Briseis (brī sē' is)   a Theban captive

Chryseis (krī sē' is)   a Theban captive

Diomedes (dī' ə mē' dēz)   a young Greek warrior

Menelaus (men' ə lā' əs)   a Greek leader, husband of Helen

Nestor (nes' tər)   a wise Greek prophet

Odysseus (ō dis' ē əs)   a clever Greek leader

Patroclus (pə trōk' ləs)   best friend to Achilles

On the Trojan side

Aeneas (i nē' əs)   a Trojan warrior, son of Aphrodite

Andromache (an drom' ə kē)   a Trojan woman, wife of Hector

Hector (hek' tər)   the greatest Trojan warrior, son of King Priam

Pandarus (pan' də rəs)   a Trojan warrior

Paris (par' is)   prince of Troy, who brought Helen to Troy

Polydorus (pol i dōr' əs)   a Trojan warrior, brother to Hector

Priam (prī' əm)   the king of Troy

46

Gods and Goddesses

Aphrodite (af rə dī′ tē)   the goddess of love and beauty, a supporter of the Trojans

Apollo (ə pol′ ō)   the god of sunlight and music, a supporter of the Trojans

Athena (ə thē′ nə)   the goddess of wisdom, a supporter of the Greeks

Hera (hir′ ə)   queen of the goddesses, wife of Zeus, and a supporter of the Greeks

Thetis (thē′ tis)   a sea-nymph, mother of Achilles

Zeus (zoos)   king of the gods, husband of Hera